GRAFFEX™

The Man in the Iron Mask

Artists: Penko Gelev
Sotir Gelev

Editor: Stephen Haynes
Editorial Assistant: Mark Williams

Published in Great Britain in 2007 by
Book House, an imprint of
The Salariya Book Company Ltd
25 Marlborough Place, Brighton, BNI IUB
www.salariya.com
www.book-house.co.uk
ISBN-13: 978-1-905638-53-6 (PB)

SALARIYA

1 3 5 7 9 8 6 4 2

A CIP catalogue record for this book is available
from the British Library.

Printed and bound in China.
Printed on paper from sustainable sources.

Visit our website at **www.book-house.co.uk**
for **free** electronic versions of:
You Wouldn't Want to be an Egyptian Mummy!
You Wouldn't Want to be a Roman Gladiator!
Avoid Joining Shackleton's Polar Expedition!
Avoid Sailing on a 19th-Century Whaling Ship!

Picture credits:
p. 42 Ann Ronan Picture Library/TopFoto/HIP
p. 43 Roger-Viollet/Topfoto
p. 45 Carolyn Franklin
p. 47 TopFoto/HIP/Photographer: Mike Newell
Every effort has been made to trace copyright holders. The Salariya Book Company apologises for any omissions and would be pleased, in such cases, to add an acknowledgement in future editions.

The Man in the Iron Mask

Alexandre Dumas

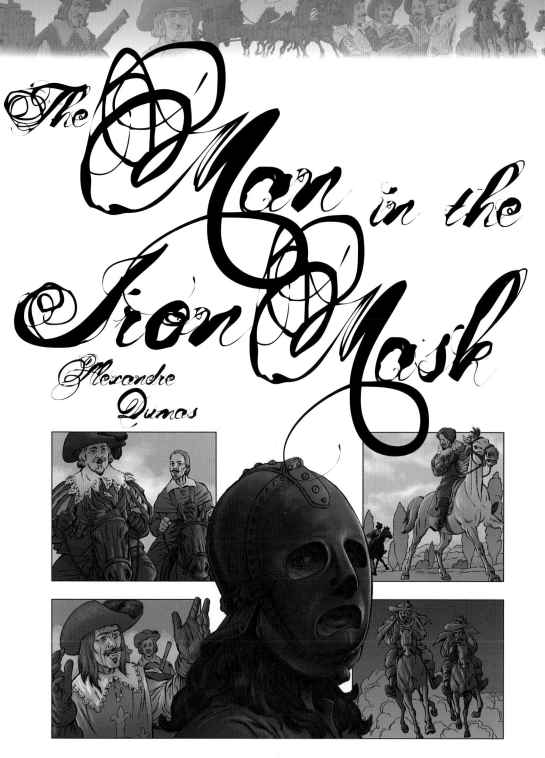

ILLUSTRATED BY

Penko Gelev

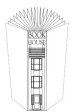

BOOK HOUSE

RETOLD BY

Jim Pipe

SERIES CREATED AND DESIGNED BY

David Salariya

'To arms!' cried Aramis.

'To arms!' thundered Porthos.

Boats filled with soldiers could be seen approaching.

'Stop them!' said Aramis. 'And if they won't stop, open fire!'

The cannon began to fire. But the boats were too close to the breakwater for the guns to hit them; they landed; fighting began practically hand to hand.

(see pages 36–37)

CHARACTERS

Aramis, Bishop of Vannes

D'Artagnan, Captain of
the King's Musketeers

Porthos,
retired musketeer

Athos, retired musketeer

Louis XIV,
King of France

Philippe,
Louis' twin brother

Queen Anne of Austria,
the King's mother

Monsieur Baisemaux,
Warden of the Bastille

Nicolas Fouquet,
Minister of Finance

Jean-Baptiste Colbert,
Chief Minister

A Visit to the Bastille

'All for one, and one for all!'

Paris, 1661

The Four Musketeers first met over 30 years ago and swore an oath of allegiance.[1] Since then, Athos and Porthos have retired and Aramis has become a bishop. But there is time for one last adventure…

Now the year is 1661. It is a starry night. Aramis, dressed in his bishop's robes, visits the infamous[2] Bastille prison in Paris. He asks to see the warden.

Follow me…

Aramis does not say a word. Instead, he gives the warden a piece of paper with a prisoner's name on it.

After a long climb, they reach the prisoner's cell.

What do you want of me?

Aramis orders the warden to leave. Inside the cell, a sad young man sits on a bed. Several plates of food lie next to him, uneaten.

Trust me. I'm an old friend.

Aramis says they have met before, when the prisoner was a boy. The young man remembers this – and a mysterious woman who visited him every month.

They said my parents were dead.

As he grew up, the boy was kept in a house surrounded by a garden with high walls. He was looked after by a nurse, Lady Perronnette, and a tutor.[3]

Your father is dead. Your mother is, too, but only to you!

Aramis warns that the young man has a powerful enemy, who sent him to the Bastille when he was fifteen.

1. oath of allegiance: a solemn promise to be loyal to one another.
2. infamous: famous for being terrible or wicked.
3. tutor: a private teacher.

THE PRISONER'S TALE

The prisoner tells Aramis what happened that day. He saw his tutor run out into the garden and look into the well.

The prisoner, then just a boy, listened as his tutor and nurse decided what to do. He heard them call him 'Philippe' – his real name.

Philippe just *had* to read that letter! While his tutor and nurse went to get a ladder, he dashed over to the well. He lowered himself to the bottom in a bucket.

Philippe plunged his hand into the icy water and grabbed the letter. Putting the two damp halves of the letter together, he read it… and discovered the amazing truth!

However, the cold water in the well gave Philippe a fever. When he talked in his sleep, his tutor found the letter, and told the Queen what had happened.

Not long after, soldiers came to the house and took Philippe away. Aramis tells Philippe they also killed his nurse and teacher.

Aramis explains that the old King, Louis XIII, waited many years for a son to succeed[1] him.

Finally, on 5 September 1638, the Queen gave birth.

1. succeed: to become king after him.

WAAAH!

While everyone celebrated, Queen Anne, who was alone with her nurse, Lady Perronnette, gave birth to another son, a twin!

Take the second boy, Nurse, and hide him!

Yes, Your Highness.

When the King heard about the twin, he was afraid that the two boys would fight for the throne when they grew up.

So the twin was taken from the palace…

We must keep the secret safe.

…and grew up in secret, cared for by the nurse and tutor. Apart from these two, and Queen Anne, no-one knew the twin existed – not even his brother!

Aramis stops talking and shows Philippe a portrait[1] of Louis XIV, the new King. Then he hands him a mirror.

No! No! I'm doomed!

When he looks into the mirror, Philippe gives a loud cry. He looks just like Louis XIV, his twin! Now he knows the King will never want to set him free.

Why did you tell me?

Because I want you to be King instead of Louis!

However, Aramis has a plan. He wants Philippe to replace his brother Louis, a useless king who cares only for fancy clothes and big feasts. When Philippe agrees, Aramis kneels down and kisses his hand. He will do everything he can to make Philippe King!

I will be back soon!

1. portrait: a painting of a person's face.

9

AN INVITATION TO THE FEAST

A few days later:

What's wrong?

I've been invited to the feast at Minister Fouquet's château...[1]

D'Artagnan, who is now Captain of the King's Musketeers, pays a visit to his old friend Porthos.

...and I've got nothing to wear!

Porthos has become too fat for his suits!

Percerin, I've brought you a client.

To cheer Porthos up, D'Artagnan takes him to the King's tailor, Master Percerin. When Percerin hears that Porthos is a friend of Fouquet, he agrees to make him a suit.

Why, it's our bishop!

Aramis arrives at Percerin's house a few minutes later. He reveals that he too has been invited to the feast at Minister Fouquet's château. D'Artagnan suspects that Aramis is up to no good.

I'm here to see the King's new suits.

Why don't you take samples of the cloth?

Aramis explains that Minister Fouquet is having a new portrait painted of King Louis. He has asked Aramis to find out what the King will be wearing at the feast, so that the picture will look exactly like him.

You will have your suit tomorrow, sir!

Porthos hates being measured, so Percerin measures his reflection instead!

1. château: a French castle or a big country house.

> Your big celebration is coming up.

> Yes, and money is running out!

> You promised me millions.

Annoyed that D'Artagnan has seen him at Percerin's house, Aramis goes to visit Minister Fouquet in his office.

Fouquet is worried. He cannot afford to pay for the big feast. He has already spent a fortune building his huge new château at Vaux-le-Vicomte.

> You'll have your money the day after the King comes to Vaux.

> The prisoner is as innocent as we are.

> What is his name?

Minister Fouquet doubts that a poor bishop like Aramis can get hold of so much money. But Aramis cannot risk telling Fouquet his plan.[1]

Aramis asks Fouquet for a letter ordering the release of a prisoner from the Bastille. He explains that the man was put in prison for criticising the Church but has now been forgiven.

> It's Seldon. He's just a child. He's been in prison for ten years.

> That's too much.

> Give this to the mother.

Aramis adds that the prisoner's mother has no money. Fouquet is taken in. Picking up a quill,[2] he quickly writes an order to free prisoner Seldon.

Aramis takes the letter. As he is about to leave, Fouquet hands him 10,000 francs[3] to give to the prisoner's mother – despite the minister's own money problems.

1. his plan: Aramis is expecting to be rewarded by Philippe when Philippe becomes King. Then he will be able to help Fouquet.
2. quill: a pen made from the cut feather of a bird.
3. francs: money formerly used in France. In the 17th century, 10 francs = 1 pistole.

THE PRISONER IS RELEASED

The great Bastille clock chimes seven. Inside the prison, the warden, Monsieur[1] Baisemeaux, is dining with Aramis in his room. This time, Aramis is dressed as a musketeer and armed with a sword.

Aramis says the room is too stuffy. He asks if the window can be opened. Secretly, he is listening out for the sound of a horseman approaching.

Several bottles of wine later, a servant comes in with a message. The warden wants to ignore it, but Aramis persuades him to read it.

It's an order to release a prisoner named Seldon. Aramis pretends to take pity on the prisoner.

When the warden gets up to call some guards, Aramis switches the release order for Seldon with one he has in his pocket. When the warden picks up the order, it has a different name on it: Marchiali.

M. Baisemeaux is confused now, and doesn't want to do anything until the next morning. However, Aramis manages to persuade the warden to free Marchiali straight away, as he is only a poor, unimportant prisoner.

1. Monsieur: the French word for Mister/Mr.

Now, monsieur, you're free!

While the warden goes to get the prisoner, Aramis snuffs out all but one of the candles in the room and waits in the shadows. Half an hour later, Baisemeaux returns with the prisoner, 'Marchiali'.

It is Philippe![1] The warden tells the prisoner he is going to be released. Looking around, Philippe suddenly sees Aramis as he walks into the light. He grabs him in delight.

Aramis leads Philippe out to his carriage and climbs in after him. He tells the driver to get going.

Aramis' heart is pounding as they make their way slowly past the huge gates of the prison. Sitting in one corner of the carriage, Philippe does not make a sound.

Once outside, the horses break into a gallop. Philippe is free!

1. Marchiali/Philippe: Philippe is called by a false name in the Bastille so that he will not be recognised. Even the warden does not know his real name.

Aramis' Plan

The carriage carrying Aramis and Philippe leaves Paris. Two hours later, it stops in the middle of the dark forest of Sénart. It is a moonless night and the two men are wrapped in darkness. All is silent except for the hoot of a nearby owl.

Louis will devour[1] the money of his people.

Aramis reveals his plan. Philippe will be switched for King Louis, a bad ruler who will ruin France. Philippe has just as much right to the throne, looks just like Louis and even has the same voice.

Tomorrow you'll sit on Louis' throne.

The following day, Philippe will take his brother's place as King, while Louis XIV will take Philippe's place in prison.

Ten minutes, and I will tell you my decision.

There are no dangers, only obstacles.

Phillipe can't believe they will get away with it, but Aramis is confident that once Louis is in prison, no-one will find out. Philippe must now choose whether to be King, or hide himself away in comfort and safety for the rest of his life.

1. devour: eat up.

Let's go! Take me to where the crown of France is!

Philippe gets out of the carriage, his legs unsteady after years in prison. Aramis waits anxiously, terrified that Philippe will choose the safer option.

Suddenly, Philippe grips Aramis' hand and agrees to go ahead with the plan. Aramis asks him if he has studied a notebook sent to him a few days before.

I've read all the notes.

How well?

I know them by heart.

Do you know the ministers?

Colbert is ugly and grumpy.

The notebook contained portraits and information about the royal family and other important people at court. Aramis tests Philippe, asking him about his mother Anne and the King's wife, Henriette.

Aramis then asks about Ministers Colbert and Fouquet. Aramis tells Philippe that Fouquet is a good man. He should be rewarded when Philippe becomes King.

What about D'Artagnan, the captain of the guards?

You will need a friend.

You're my only friend.

Aramis explains that though D'Artagnan is a good friend, he will fight for King Louis, so nothing must be said to him until the switch has taken place.

Finally, Philippe asks Aramis to be his Prime Minister in return for helping him to become King. Aramis refuses, but asks Philippe to help him get elected as Pope!

THE FEAST AT VAUX

15 August. Minister Fouquet's château at Vaux-le-Vicomte is abuzz with servants preparing for a magnificent feast.

Hurry up. His Majesty will be here soon!

Cheer up, Fouquet!

Believe it or not, the King hardly likes me at all!

Inside the château, Aramis and Fouquet admire the new portrait of King Louis. Fouquet is feeling very nervous about the arrival of the King. Aramis teases him about his rivalry with Minister Colbert.

Where are you staying?

In the Blue Chamber. [1]

When Aramis mentions where he is sleeping, Fouquet asks him to keep quiet, as he will be right above the King's bedroom, the Gold Chamber.

What is Aramis after?

As Captain of the King's Musketeers, D'Artagnan is also at Vaux. He is suspicious of Aramis' friendship with Fouquet.

7 o'clock: King Louis arrives at the château.

He is met by a spectacular firework display.

1. chamber: bedroom.

Even the plates are made of gold!

An hour later, other carriages arrive carrying Queen Anne, the King's ministers and other nobles, courtiers and ladies. They sit down to a grand banquet. The courtiers wolf down the food. D'Artagnan stuffs his face!

Looking at Fouquet's beautiful château and the incredible feast in front of him, the King is mad with envy.

Is Your Majesty ready for his servants?

No: first I need a chat with Colbert.

ZZZZzzzz...

So here we all are at Vaux!

In a sulk, the King stomps back to his room, the Gold Chamber. When Fouquet asks if anything is the matter, the King pretends to be sleepy.

While the King is in his chamber, D'Artagnan can visit Aramis. Entering the room, he sees Porthos sitting in a chair and snoring loudly. D'Artagnan is happy to be back among his old musketeer friends.

Why did you take those samples from Percerin?

What do you suspect?

Sssh! You'll wake the King with your heavy footsteps.

D'Artagnan is amazed to see how much money Fouquet has spent on the banquet. But he also thinks Aramis is behaving suspiciously. He aks him if he is plotting against the King.

Aramis pretends to be angry, saying he would never hurt the true King of France.[1] D'Artagnan believes him and leaves the room, taking a yawning Porthos with him.

1. the true King of France: the others think he means Louis, but secretly he means Philippe.

Spying on the King

After D'Artagnan and Porthos have left the room, Philippe crawls out from his secret hiding place. He is worried that D'Artagnan may get in their way.

Aramis slides back part of the floor. He shows Philippe an opening which will allow him to watch the King and copy the way he moves and talks.

Philippe looks down and sees his brother Louis for the first time. The King is talking with Minister Colbert.

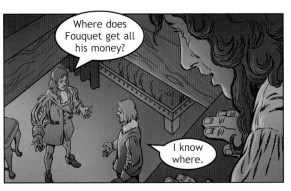

As Aramis and Philippe listen, the King asks Colbert how Fouquet can afford this new château and the splendid feast. Colbert tells him Fouquet has stolen 13 million francs from the King's treasury.[1]

Colbert wants the King to send Fouquet to prison. But the King feels bad about arresting Fouquet in his own home.

The King decides to deal with the matter the next day. Colbert is secretly delighted that Fouquet is going to be arrested.

As Colbert leaves, the King calls his servants. Above them, Philippe is about to look away when Aramis stops him.

Aramis tells Philippe to watch and learn exactly how the King behaves as he gets ready for bed.

1. treasury: a place where treasure or money is stored.

The guests at Vaux are again treated to a lavish feast, music, fireworks and plays. But nothing cheers up Louis, even when he wins at cards. He is too busy thinking about what to do with Minister Fouquet.

That evening, Louis sends for D'Artagnan. Again, Aramis and Philippe listen through the opening in the floor.

D'Artagnan is very reluctant to arrest Minister Fouquet. Worried that the King may change his mind later, he asks Louis to give him a written order.

Louis is furious at D'Artagnan, but he realises that Fouquet must not be arrested in public. So for the time being he just tells D'Artagnan to watch Fouquet carefully.

Louis asks D'Artagnan to leave, then flies into a jealous rage.

In his anger, Louis knocks over a table, then collapses on his bed, weeping. Still fully dressed, he falls into a deep sleep.

KIDNAP!

This is just a dream. Wake up!

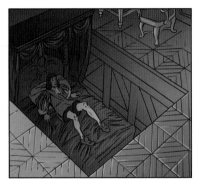

Louis tosses and turns in his bed. In the middle of the night, he imagines seeing his own face staring down from the ceiling.

How could he guess that it is his brother Philippe watching him?

Louis feels the bed sinking into the floor! He wakes up – only to find that he hasn't been dreaming after all!

All you need to know is that we're in charge!

Is this a joke?

I'm not budging!

If you struggle, I'll roll you up in a cloak and carry you!

Amazingly, the bed has sunk down into a cold, dark room. Two men are standing over the bed, each dressed in a long cloak. Their faces are covered by masks.

Louis jumps up. Stamping his foot, he demands to know who the two men are. In the dim light of the lantern, he can see that the walls are wet and covered in the slime from crawling slugs.

Is this a dungeon?

No. It's an underground passage.

Louis realises he has no choice but to go with the two masked men. They march him along a long, winding corridor until they reach a heavy door. One of his captors takes out a key and opens the door.

Get in!

The door leads outside. Here a carriage waits under the trees. One man gets into the carriage with the King. The other climbs into the driver's seat.

The carriage flies through the night, arriving at the Bastille at 3 o'clock the next morning. But who are the masked men? It is Porthos and Aramis!

What's this about?

One sound and I'll shoot you!

My mistake. I'm bringing him back.

Porthos tells the guard to wake the warden, who comes to the gate in his dressing gown.

Porthos climbs into the carriage and points a gun at the King. Then Aramis gets out, taking off his mask.

Aramis tells the warden there has been a mistake. The other day he took away the wrong prisoner – Marchiali instead of Seldon.

Just lock him up right now. He's insane.

Aramis explains that Marchiali thinks he is the King. He should not be allowed to speak to anyone. The King is now thrown into the cell once occupied by Philippe.

With no time to waste, Aramis and Porthos are soon back on the road to Vaux.

THE NEW KING

When Louis sees a large rat in his cell, he's horrified. He calls out, but no one replies. In frustration, Louis smashes a chair against his cell door.

Then he calls out of his cell window. The other prisoners tell him to keep quiet.

When a guard finally appears, he tells the King he is mad. Louis flies into an even greater rage, jumping from the table and rattling the window bars in his cell.

The guard warns Louis that he will be put in an even worse dungeon if he does not behave.

Meanwhile, back at Vaux:

Fouquet is exhausted after two days of looking after his guests. D'Artagnan does not want to arrest him, but explains that he has orders to guard Fouquet.

D'Artagnan pretends to go and look for Aramis. He knows Fouquet will use this time to destroy any evidence against him.

Once he is alone, Fouquet grabs letters and documents from their secret hiding place and burns them.

Meanwhile:

Philippe, this is your destiny![1]

Philippe lies in Louis' bed, pretending to sleep. The night before, he was lowered into the King's room, just as the King was lowered into the secret passage below.

Sire,[2] everything is done!

Does the warden suspect anything?

Not a thing!

Aramis creeps into the room and wakes Philippe. He tells him that everything has gone to plan. In a few days' time Louis will be smuggled out of the Bastille and sent far away .

Porthos will die of happiness!

Philippe says he will make Porthos a duke in thanks for his help. Aramis bursts out laughing, knowing how happy this will make Porthos.

Their laughter is cut short by a loud knock at the door. It is D'Artagnan.

Let's attack him!

Oh no — D'Artagnan knows nothing.

Aramis warns Philippe not to talk to D'Artagnan yet, as he might be suspicious.

You? Here?

D'Artagnan is shocked to see Aramis in the King's chamber, where only the most important people are allowed.

His Majesty needs some more sleep!

However, Aramis persuades D'Artagnan that the King is tired and does not want to see anyone. He then gives D'Artagnan a written order to free Fouquet.

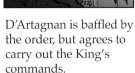

I don't understand!

D'Artagnan is baffled by the order, but agrees to carry out the King's commands.

1. destiny: something that is bound to happen to you, because of fate.
2. sire: an old-fashioned way of saying 'sir'.

FOUQUET LEARNS ALL

You've brought me Aramis?

No, I bring freedom!

How did you become the King's favourite?

We've met hundreds of times.

Aramis and D'Artagnan go to see Minister Fouquet. D'Artagnan tells Fouquet he will not be arresting him. In fact, the King has asked him to thank Fouquet for the feast. Fouquet is surprised.

As he is about to go, D'Artagnan asks Aramis how he got so close to the King. Aramis explains that he has met the King many times – but in secret.

What's going on, Aramis?

Colbert told the King you were a thief.

One twin was lucky, the other miserable.

Aramis, you're scaring me!

Once D'Artagnan has left, Aramis tells Fouquet he was accused of stealing from the Treasury. Fouquet suspects Aramis is hiding something from him.

Aramis decides to let Fouquet in on the secret. He tells him of the twin brothers, and how they look so alike.

Yesterday's King is in the Bastille. I kidnapped him.

It's a crime, an abominable[1] crime!

I am a man of honour!

Fouquet cannot bear to hear any more. He buries his face in his hands. He realises that Aramis wants him to join the conspiracy. Fouquet cannot believe that Aramis has kidnapped the King in his house.

Fouquet gets more and more angry. Aramis can't understand why he supports the King, even though the King wanted to arrest him.

1. abominable: disgusting, hateful.

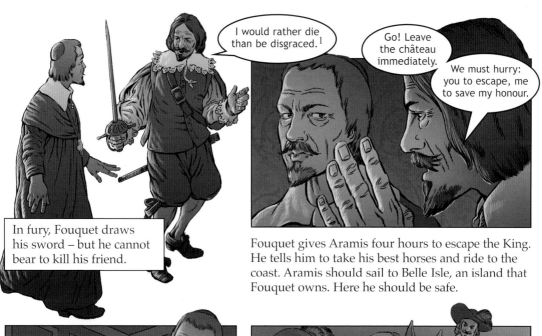

I would rather die than be disgraced.[1]

Go! Leave the château immediately.

We must hurry: you to escape, me to save my honour.

In fury, Fouquet draws his sword – but he cannot bear to kill his friend.

Fouquet gives Aramis four hours to escape the King. He tells him to take his best horses and ride to the coast. Aramis should sail to Belle Isle, an island that Fouquet owns. Here he should be safe.

Wake up! We're going on a secret mission.

Those two are running from something!

Goodbye, old friend!

Without Fouquet's help, Aramis' plan has failed. He decides to leave Philippe behind – he was a prisoner before, and will stay a prisoner. Aramis goes to find Porthos.

Aramis and Porthos are about to leave when D'Artagnan appears. Aramis is forced to lie to him. He tells D'Artagnan that Fouquet has left the château and that he and Porthos have to leave on the King's business.

D'Artagnan helps Aramis onto his horse, and the two friends gallop away.

1. be disgraced: Fouquet is ashamed because the plot was carried out in his house, while the King was his guest. The King should have been safe there.

FOUQUET FREES THE KING

Fouquet's carriage tears along the road to Paris and soon arrives at the Bastille. At first, the guards don't recognise the Minister. They refuse to let him in.

I'm the King's Minister, you fools!

Fouquet tries to push past the guards and starts a fight.

Forgive me, please!

I could have you drawn and quartered for this![1]

I want a word in private.

Hearing the noise, the warden arrives. He recognises Fouquet and tells his men to let him in. Fouquet follows the warden to his room.

Fouquet finds out that Aramis has been to the Bastille twice, taking and then bringing back a prisoner called Marchiali.

Take me to the prisoner this instant!

Fouquet demands to see 'Marchiali'. The warden complains about the prisoner's fits of rage.

For pity's sake, sir!

I'll smash down your gates! Just you wait and see!

Help! I'm the King!

BANG! BANG! BANG!

At first the warden refuses to let Fouquet see the prisoner without an order from the King. But when Fouquet threatens to attack the prison with 10,000 men and 30 cannons, the warden gives in.

As they walk along the prison corridors, they can hear the wild screams of the King. Fouquet takes the keys to the King's cell from the warden.

1. drawn and quartered: traitors were punished by being hung by the neck. Then their insides were ripped out (drawn), and finally their bodies were chopped into pieces (quartered).

The door opens. Fouquet is shocked by the terrible state of the King. His shirt is torn and his chest and arms are bloody.

The King is terrified that Fouquet wants to kill him. Fouquet calms him, telling him that he has come to set him free.

Fouquet tells Louis about Aramis' plot. But the King refuses to believe him.

Fouquet explains that because 'Marchiali' (Philippe) has exactly the same face as the King, even his own mother Queen Anne would have been taken in by him.

The King orders Fouquet to assemble all the soldiers in Paris at the prison, then go with him to Vaux to kill the traitors.

Fouquet pleads for Aramis and Porthos. But when Louis finds out that they are heading for Belle Isle, he orders his musketeers to go there and kill them.

Fouquet gets Louis to sign a new release order, and leads him out of the prison. Watching them leave, the warden tears his hair out. He can't understand what's going on with this prisoner Marchiali!

1. viper: a type of poisonous snake; also a name for a treacherous person.

THE FALSE KING

Later that morning:

What do you think of Monsieur Fouquet now?

You must treat him like a friend.

Philippe is acting the part of the King well. None of the servants suspect him. He asks to see Queen Anne. He wants to love his mother, despite what she has allowed to happen to him. But will she notice any difference between him and his brother?

Why are you being so cruel?

But he secretly forgives her for the harm she has done.

Philippe tells Queen Anne that he wants to banish her friend for plotting with Colbert against Fouquet.

What does Your Majesty wish?

Where is Aramis? Please find him.

Then D'Artagnan arrives. Philippe asks him to find Aramis so that he can introduce him to the Queen. D'Artagnan is confused: he last saw Aramis and Porthos going off on a secret mission for the King.

GASP!

Suddenly, there is a commotion outside the door. They hear Fouquet's voice. But when the door opens, King Louis walks in!

The Queen screams in shock, as if seeing a ghost. Louis and Philippe stare at each other, trembling. Seeing Philippe, Fouquet realises that he should have helped Aramis after all. D'Artagnan's eyes pop out of his head in amazement.

Louis dashes to the shutters and opens them, then tears down the curtain. Light floods into the room. Philippe steps back into the shadows.

Both Louis and Philippe turn to Queen Anne to decide which of them is the true King. Anne is so shocked at seeing the two of them together that she collapses in a chair.

Louis appeals to D'Artagnan. He points out that the pretender[1] has been in a dark prison, while the real King has been out in the sun.

D'Artagnan looks at Philippe's pale face. In his mind, there is no doubt. He walks over and arrests Philippe, who does not resist.

Though her own son is about to be led away, Queen Anne does nothing to help him.

A few minutes later, Colbert hands D'Artagnan a written order from the King. He must take Philippe to the fort on the island of Sainte-Marguerite.

D'Artagnan shudders as he reads the order: Philippe's face is to be covered with an iron mask so that no-one will ever see it again!

Philippe resigns himself to his fate and goes with D'Artagnan.

1. pretender: a person who claims to be King.

ATHOS AND RAOUL

Aramis and Porthos race to the coast. Porthos is still unsure why they had to leave Vaux, but he trusts Aramis. By night they are at Blois, 250 km from Vaux.

Their horses are tired. Aramis suggests they visit their old musketeer friend, Athos, who lives nearby.

Athos is out in the garden with his son Raoul when Aramis and Porthos arrive. Porthos tells them that the King wants to make him a duke.

Athos is surprised by this, so Aramis tells him the truth about the failed plot, and the danger he and Porthos now face. Porthos still doesn't know about the plot.[1]

Athos refuses to join Aramis and Porthos, but lends them his two best horses. He feels very sad to see them go.

Soon after, Athos and Raoul leave for Paris, determined to find out more from D'Artagnan.

D'Artagnan has left Paris. But, talking to his faithful servant Planchet, they discover the map he used to plan his route.

The pinholes in the map show D'Artagnan's route to the port of Toulon on the south coast.

Athos and Raoul cross France, riding 15 leagues[2] a day. It takes them two weeks to reach Toulon.

1. Porthos doesn't know: he thinks the person they arrested at Vaux-le-Vicomte and took to the Bastille was an impostor, not the real King.
2. league: the distance a person could walk in an hour – about 5 km or 3 miles.

In Toulon, a fisherman tells how he was forced to rent his boat to a mysterious gentleman and ferry a coach past the dangerous reefs to Sainte-Marguerite.

When the crew refused to go on, a man with a hideous mask stepped out of the coach and shook his fist at them. In terror, they jumped into the sea.

Athos and Raoul hire a boat and sail to the island of Sainte-Marguerite.

As they approach the fort, a silver plate is hurled from one of the barred windows.

Raoul picks up the dusty plate and finds a message scratched on it.

Just then a bullet whizzes by, close to Raoul's head. A group of eight soldiers come running out of the fort.

Athos and Raoul are about to jump into the moat for safety when D'Artagnan, leading the soldiers, tells his men to lower their arms.

Afraid that they will be killed for finding out about Philippe, D'Artagnan wipes the message from the plate with his sword.

He tells them to pretend to be Spanish and not to understand what is going on.

THE MAN IN THE IRON MASK

Later that day:

Look: the prisoner is coming back from the chapel.[1]

D'Artagnan explains that the secret of the King's brother must not be revealed to anyone. Suddenly, pushing the other two into a corner, he points upward.

A man walks six paces behind the prison governor. His head is completely covered by an iron helmet. The prisoner stops and looks up at the sky.

He sighs so heavily, it sounds like a roar.

There goes an unhappy man!

Next day:

Meanwhile:

I must be careful. My enemies are powerful and my friends cannot help me.

As the iron door swings shut on the prisoner's cell, the three men look on sadly. There is no escape for poor Philippe.

Athos and Raoul leave for home. D'Artagnan is ordered to go to Nantes, on the west coast, with a brigade of soldiers. Will the King force him to attack Belle Isle?

Fouquet is called to Nantes to meet the King. Little does he know that Colbert has already plotted his downfall.

You'll arrest Fouquet and lock him up!

D'Artagnan gives chase.

Stop in the name of the King!

I must catch Fouquet, or people will say I've been paid to let him escape!

When D'Artagnan arrives in Nantes, the King tells him to arrest Fouquet. Fouquet hears of this, and tries to escape.

1. chapel: a church which is part of the fort.

"I'll catch him even if it kills my horse!"

Slowly but surely, D'Artagnan catches up with Fouquet.

"I am your prisoner, sir. Take my arm, you're about to faint!"

D'Artagnan's horse collapses with exhaustion. Just as it falls, D'Artagnan shoots and wounds Fouquet's horse with his pistol. Realising he cannot escape, Fouquet dismounts[1] and D'Artagnan arrests him.

"This coach wasn't thought up by a good man like you, D'Artagnan."

D'Artagnan locks Fouquet in a special coach with a grille over the windows so he cannot drop any secret messages out.

"How dare Colbert ask **my** men to smash up Fouquet's house!"

"Don't speak like that in front of me."

Later, D'Artagnan discovers that Colbert has ordered the King's musketeers to arrest Fouquet's family and friends and destroy his property. Hiding his fury, he asks the King to spare Fouquet.

"Why are you not guarding Fouquet?"

"Don't come back until you have the keys to Belle Isle."

"I left him with my stupidest captain in the hope that he would escape!"

D'Artagnan tells the King he should be grateful to Fouquet for setting him free.

The King does not care. He orders D'Artagnan to go to Belle Isle with 200 men to capture it.

"It won't be easy to climb over your friend's corpse!"[2]

As D'Artagnan leaves, Colbert sneers at him. He knows D'Artagnan is being sent to kill his best friends.

1. dismounts: gets off his horse.
2. corpse: dead body.

D'Artagnan's Plan

The beach at Belle Isle:

Porthos sees seven ships approaching.

The King's men have come to attack them! Aramis tells Porthos to warn the islanders so they can defend themselves. The ships come nearer. They anchor, and a small boat is lowered into the water.

When the boat arrives at the beach, a young man jumps out. Aramis recognises him as Jonathas, a local fisherman who had been captured by the King's men.

Jonathas brings a letter from D'Artagnan telling Aramis that he has been ordered to capture Belle Isle and that Fouquet has been put in the Bastille.

Aramis looks at the letter again. The handwriting has been forged! Aramis suspects a trap.

Aramis refuses to meet D'Artagnan unless he comes to the island in person. Jonathas takes this message back to D'Artagnan.

As they walk towards the fort, Aramis at last explains to Porthos about the plot to replace the King with his brother.

Porthos finally realises why he was going to be made a duke, and why they are now being hunted by D'Artagnan and his musketeers.[1]

They spot D'Artagnan arriving at the harbour. He is with one of the King's officers, who has orders to follow and observe him in case he tries to let his friends escape.

D'Artagnan is furious, but persuades the officer to allow him to speak in private to Aramis and Porthos.

D'Artagnan tells them they are surrounded. He won't obey the King's orders to kill them, but they must come and talk to the King.

Aramis asks D'Artagnan to take Porthos with him, because he is innocent. When Porthos refuses to go, D'Artagnan tells them he has a plan, then goes back to his ship.

1. why he was going to be made a duke... : it was Philippe who was going to make him a duke, to thank the musketeers for making him King. Now that Louis is back on the throne, Aramis and Porthos are outlaws.

THE ATTACK ON BELLE ISLE

"Read this, Monsieur."

"The King no longer trusts me. I resign!"

"Let's come to an agreement with them."

D'Artagnan tells his men that the locals will defend the island – even against the King. He advises them to meet with two local officers (he means Porthos and Aramis).

But the King's officer hands D'Artagnan an order from the King. It tells him not to bring any officers to the ships.

D'Artagnan has one last trick: he resigns. He tells his men to return to Nantes so the King can appoint a new captain.

"Louis is as cunning as that old fox Richelieu![1]"

"The minute you resign, you are to be arrested!"

The King's officer hands D'Artagnan another order. D'Artagnan's face goes pale as he reads it.

D'Artagnan is now a prisoner. His only hope is to reach Nantes and plead with the King.

As D'Artagnan sails to the mainland, he hears the boom of cannon.

"We'll sail at night. We'll reach Spain in twelve hours."

"Porthos, we need a prisoner. Hurry!"

Realising that D'Artagnan's plan has failed and the attack has begun, Aramis and Porthos plan their escape. They will sail to Spain using a small boat hidden inside the Locmaria cave on Belle Isle.

A short while later, Aramis sees a fleet of small boats heading for the beach, too close for his cannon to hit them. The King's men are about to land! Aramis tells Porthos to take one of them prisoner.

1. Richelieu: the scheming Cardinal Richelieu, Chief Minister to King Louis XIII, was an enemy of the musketeers in their earlier adventures.

Aramis warns the islanders to arm themselves. A few minutes later, the fighting begins.

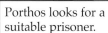

Porthos looks for a suitable prisoner.

The King's men are forced back.

You are to be killed in the attack or hanged later.

Aramis and Porthos ask the prisoner what the King has in store for them. But suddenly they hear the sound of gunfire from the other side of the island.

Into the fort, everyone!

Put down your weapons. Return to your homes in peace.

They have been tricked! More of the King's soldiers have landed on the far side of the island. Soon, all the islanders are running back into the fort for safety.

Inside the fort, Aramis tells the islanders that Fouquet has been arrested and put in the Bastille. He persuades them not to fight. The islanders are surprised, but agree to do as Aramis tells them.

ESCAPE!

When it is dark, Aramis and Porthos cross the island to reach the Locmaria cave. Here a boat and three friendly local fishermen wait for them.

Aramis enters the cave.

Inside the cave they see the three fishermen waiting by a small boat. At the other end of the cave is an opening to the sea.

Soon it will be dawn – they must hurry. But just as the men are about to launch the boat, they hear dogs barking nearby.

The King's men are closing in! The dogs lead them into the cave. There are sixteen of them against two musketeers!

Aramis and Porthos get ready to ambush their enemies. They hide behind a rock.

Twice the thunder of muskets booms in the cave.

Soon ten of the King's men are dead.

More soldiers arrive. When they hear that the two men defending the cave are the famous musketeers Porthos and Aramis, they are afraid. But their captain urges them to attack.

1. Monseigneur: My Lord. This is the correct way to address a bishop in French.

At the other end of the cave, the three fishermen roll the boat towards the sea. But a giant rock blocks the way.

Only the mighty Porthos can move it.

Porthos and Aramis are about the launch the boat when they hear the King's men coming. Porthos seizes an iron bar.

THWACK!

UUR GH!

THUNK!

With ten giant blows he kills another ten men by cracking their skulls.

Porthos' huge paw reaches out and grabs the captain by the neck. Soon he is dead. Another officer orders the men to open fire. Confused and barely able to see in the darkness of the cave, they shoot each other!

THE END OF THE MUSKETEERS

Go on, light the fuse!

The fight is not over yet. A third and final wave of the King's soldiers enters the cave. Aramis has prepared a large barrel of gunpowder. Porthos tells him to run for safety, then picks up the barrel. He is so excited, he cannot help laughing!

For a brief moment, Porthos' pale face is lit up by the fuse. Then he hurls the barrel.

BOOM!

The barrel flies 30 paces through the air. The King's men see it coming, but it's too late. The barrel explodes, bringing down the roof of the cave.

But Porthos' old legs cannot carry him fast enough out of harm's way. He is trapped by a giant block of stone.

Porthos! Porthos!

It's... too... heavy!

The others do all they can to lift off the enormous rock, but it is too heavy for them. Brave Porthos dies with a final gasp.

As the little boat sails for Spain, Aramis' eyes fill with tears.

Noble Porthos — the toughest musketeer, but the first to die!

Back in Nantes:

We lost 106 men.

D'Artagnan defends his actions to the King. A messenger arrives, telling them that Belle Isle has been captured.

Will you vouch for them?[1]

With my life.

The King begs D'Artagnan not to resign from the musketeers. D'Artagnan accepts, but only if the King will forgive the people of Belle Isle. The King agrees.

D'Artagnan visits the Locmaria cave…

…but does not find Porthos' body.

Back in Paris:

Don't worry. Aramis will stay a free man.

D'Artagnan receives a letter from Aramis. Thanks to Colbert's spies, the King has read it already.

This was the final adventure of the four musketeers. A year later, Athos dies of grief when he hears that his son Raoul has been killed fighting in Spain.

Another four years on, an aging D'Artagnan dies fighting for Louis XIV against the Dutch. He is leading an attack on a fortress when he is struck in the chest by a flying cannonball.

Athos, Porthos, goodbye! Aramis, goodbye forever!

As D'Artagnan lies dying, his last thoughts are of his three musketeer friends.

Now, only Aramis is left of the four musketeers. Never again will he hear the cry: 'All for one, and one for all!'

1. vouch for them: promise that they will behave themselves.

The End 41

Alexandre Dumas was born on 24 July 1802 in Villers-Cotterêts, north of Paris. His father, Thomas-Alexandre Dumas, was the son of a French nobleman and a black slave who met in the French colony of Santo Domingo (now called Haiti). Back in France, Thomas-Alexandre became a general under Napoleon Bonaparte, but fell out with Napoleon. He died in poverty when Alexandre was only four, so Alexandre and his mother moved in with her parents, the Labourets, who ran the Hôtel de l'Épée.

EARLY SUCCESSES

Dumas grew up in Villers-Cotterêts, spending many hours in the forest with his friends Hanniquet and Boudoux, the local poachers. He was taught by his mother and then by the village priest before becoming a clerk for a local lawyer. In 1823, aged 20, he went to Paris to find fame and fortune. Dumas got a job working for the Duc d'Orléans (later King Louis Philippe), but soon found his way into the world of theatre and publishing. By 1829, he had made a name for himself with the play *Henry III and his Court*, performed by the celebrated Comédie Française, the French national theatre.

A FAMOUS PLAYWRIGHT

At first, Dumas was famous for his plays rather than for his novels. In 1832, he wrote the hugely successful play *The Tower of Nesle*. This was actually a rewrite of a work by Frédéric Gaillardet.

Alexandre Dumas père, photographed by Nadar in about 1855

Gaillardet was so upset when Dumas took the credit for the rewrite that he challenged him to a duel with pistols. Luckily, neither man hit the other! Dumas wrote hundreds of plays during his lifetime, as well as travel diaries, children's stories and a dictionary of food. He also wrote for several weekly magazines.

THE BIG SPENDER

This incredible stream of work earned Dumas over 200,000 francs a year – an enormous sum in those days. However, he lived just like the heroes of his books, spending huge sums on extravagant parties and good living.

In his lifetime he made and lost several fortunes. At 1.88m (6ft 2in) tall, he was also a man of action, taking part in the French Revolution of 1830. He caught cholera in the great epidemic of 1832, but survived.

His novels
Dumas went to Italy to recover from the disease, where he married the actress Ida Ferrier in 1840. However, they soon broke up after he had spent all her money. Around this time, Dumas turned to writing novels, and over the next 30 years he wrote some 250 books, helped by over 70 assistants. These were often published as serials, with a new chapter each week. Among his most famous novels are *The Three Musketeers*, *The Count of Monte Cristo* and *The Vicomte of Bragelonne* (the last volume of which is *The Man in the Iron Mask*).

Dumas' travels
By 1852, Dumas was bankrupt again and was forced to flee to Brussels, in Belgium. He returned to Paris three years later, then began a new set of adventures, travelling to England, Germany, Russia and finally Italy, where he helped Garibaldi during the War of Italian Unification. From 1861 to 1864 he lived in Naples, in the south of Italy, before setting off again on tours of Austria, Hungary and Spain. In 1870, Dumas finally settled down in his son's villa in northern France, where he died on 5 December, after a life filled with writing, travelling and partying.

In the family
Alexandre's son, Alexandre Dumas junior, followed in his literary footsteps, writing many plays and several important novels, including *The Lady of the Camellias*. The elder Dumas is often referred to as 'Dumas père' (French for 'Dumas the father') to avoid confusion with his son.

Dumas' reputation
Many of Dumas' works are historical novels mixing fact with fiction. Critics accused him of distorting the truth, but his fans loved his ability to write great action stories and create larger-than-life characters. Overseas, his works were particularly popular among 19th-century African-Americans, though in public Dumas did not refer much to his African ancestry. The Scottish writer Robert Louis Stevenson – himself famous for gripping adventure stories such as *Treasure Island* and *Kidnapped* – read *The Vicomte of Bragelonne* six times and described it as his 'favourite book'.

An illustration from an early edition of The Three Musketeers

The Man in the Iron Mask was not intended as a book to be read on its own. It was the final volume of Dumas' novel *The Vicomte of Bragelonne: Ten Years Later*, which is itself the third part of the historical epic that begins with *The Three Musketeers*. It appeared as a serial between October 1847 and January 1850 in the popular Paris paper, *Le Siècle* (*The Century*).

The book was not written as a whole, but in chapters, some hammered out just a few days or even hours before they were to be printed. Despite the amazing speed at which Dumas wrote, *The Three Musketeers* and the following parts of the epic, including *The Man in the Iron Mask*, became instantly popular. Queues formed in the streets to buy the newspaper carrying the latest episode.

Unlike most authors, Dumas constantly worked on several different projects at the same time, organised by a system of colour coding: his novels were written on blue paper, his plays on yellow and his magazine articles on pink paper!

FACT AND FICTION

As with all his historical novels, Dumas used a team of researchers to work on *The Man in the Iron Mask*. His main collaborator was a young history teacher, Auguste Maquet. However, Dumas first got the idea for the musketeer novels himself after reading *The Memoirs of D'Artagnan* by Gatien Courtilz de Sandras (1644–1712), which told the rather boring tale of an officer in Louis XIII's army. In fact, all four of his famous musketeers – Aramis, Porthos, Athos and D'Artagnan – were partly based on real people, as are King Louis XIV, Fouquet and Colbert.

Dumas' and Maquet's skill was to make these historical figures into larger-than-life characters, creating amazing adventures for them and bringing them to life with fast-moving dialogue. The idea of Porthos as a strongman came from Dumas' own father, General Thomas-Alexandre Dumas, who could lift huge barn doors off their hinges single-handed!

THE REAL MAN IN THE MASK?

Did the Man in the Iron Mask really exist? There was certainly no plot to replace Louis XIV, and he never had a twin brother. Some historians believe it was D'Artagnan himself who was locked up in a velvet mask. However, the myth of the Iron Mask may have been made up 100 years later by Mirabeau, one of the leaders of the French Revolution of 1789. After an angry mob stormed the hated Bastille prison, Mirabeau felt that visitors would like to see more than just empty rooms. An old suit of armour was wrapped around a skeleton to make it look like an 'iron corset' – an instrument of torture designed to squeeze its victim to death. In a country filled with hatred for the royal family, people were quick to believe in the cruel story of 'The Man in the Iron Mask'.

PLACES IN THE STORY

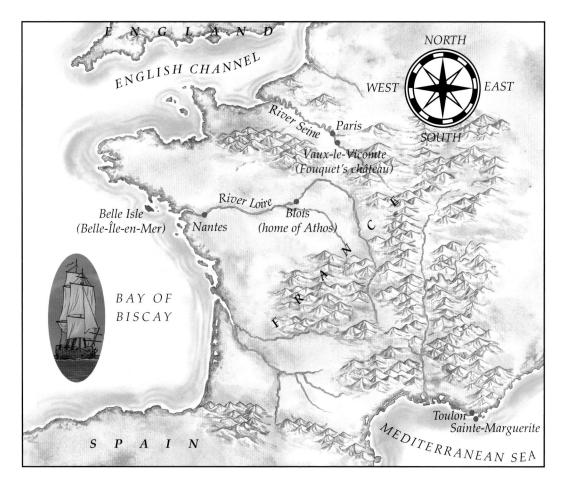

OTHER NOVELS BY DUMAS PÈRE

Here are the English titles of Dumas'
most famous novels, with the dates when
they were first published in French.

1838   *Captain Paul*
1844   *The Three Musketeers*
1844–1845 *The Count of Monte Cristo*
1846   *Twenty Years After* (sequel to *The
        Three Musketeers*)
1847   *Queen Margot*
1847–1850 *The Vicomte of Bragelonne,
        Louise de la Vallière* and *The Man
        in the Iron Mask* (second sequel
        to *The Three Musketeers*)

1848   *The Forty-Five Guardsmen*
1851   *The Black Tulip*
1852   *Conscience*
1853   *Taking the Bastille*
1860   *Black: The Story of a Dog*

IMPORTANT EVENTS

IN THE LIFETIME OF ALEXANDRE DUMAS PÈRE

1802
24th July: Dumas is born in Villers-Cotterêts, France.
French Revolutionary Wars end.

1803
Louisiana Purchase: US doubles in size after buying land from France for $15 million.

1804
Napoleon proclaims himself emperor of France.

1808
Beethoven's Fifth Symphony is first performed.

1815
Napoleon is finally defeated at Waterloo.

1819
Simón Bolívar liberates New Granada (now Colombia, Venezuela and Ecuador) from Spain.

1822
Greece declares independence from Turkey.

1825
First passenger-carrying railway in England.

1826
Oldest surviving photograph is taken by Joseph-Nicéphore Niepce (France).

1829
Dumas becomes a leader of the Romantic movement with his play *Henry III and his Court*.

1833
Slavery is abolished in the British Empire.

1834
Charles Babbage (UK) invents mechanical adding machine, a forerunner of computers.

1836
Boer farmers in southern Africa start the 'Great Trek', founding republics in Natal, Transvaal and Orange Free State.

1844
Samuel F. B. Morse (US) invents the telegraph.

1846
US declares war on Mexico (war lasts until 1849).
Failure of potato crop causes famine in Ireland.

1847
Dumas begins writing *The Vicomte of Bragelonne*, which contains the *Man in the Iron Mask* story.

1848
Revolutions across Europe. In France, Louis Napoléon is elected President of the Republic.
Karl Marx and Friedrich Engels (Germany/UK) publish the *Communist Manifesto*.

1849
Thousands rush to California in search of gold.

1851
Herman Melville (US) writes *Moby-Dick*.

1853
Crimean War begins between Russia and Turkey, France, and Britain (war lasts until 1856).
US Commodore Perry reaches Tokyo; Japan is forced to trade with the outside world.

1856
Gustave Flaubert (France) writes *Madame Bovary*.

1857
India becomes part of the British Empire.
First transatlantic telegraph cable.

1859
Work begins on Suez Canal (completed 1869).
Unification of Italy begins under Count Cavour.
Jean-Joseph-Étienne Lenoir (Belgium) builds the first internal combustion engine.
Charles Darwin (UK) publishes *On the Origin of Species*, setting out his theory of evolution.

1861
American Civil War begins.
Kingdom of Italy is proclaimed under Piedmontese King Victor Emmanuel II.
Louis Pasteur (France) discovers bacteria.

1865
American Civil War ends; slavery is banned.
US President Abraham Lincoln is assassinated.

1866
Alfred Nobel (Sweden) invents dynamite.
Austria is defeated by Prussia and Italy in the Seven Weeks' War.

1867
US buys Alaska from Russia for $7.2 million.

1868
Revolution in Spain.

1870
Franco-Prussian war begins (ends 1871).
5th December: Alexandre Dumas dies in Puys, near Dieppe, France.

STAGE AND SCREEN

ADAPTATIONS OF *THE MAN IN THE IRON MASK*

The story of *The Man in the Iron Mask* has been made into films and adapted for TV on many occasions in the past 80 years. However, the story was first told in a play by Alexandre Dumas himself, in collaboration with Narcisse Fournier and Auguste Arnould. This stage version has only been discovered very recently, and we do not know whether it was performed in Dumas' day.

The first film version was made in 1929. It was the last silent film starring the legendary actor Douglas Fairbanks senior, who played D'Artagnan. A second version was filmed in 1939 by director James Whale. Like most film versions, it changed the plot around, so that the four musketeers fight against the evil mastermind Fouquet. It also has King Louis XIV hoping that Philippe's beard will grow so long inside the iron mask that it strangles him!

Later films follow the 1939 plot rather than the book, so that Philippe successfully assumes the throne and Louis ends up wearing the iron mask in prison. In the 1998 movie Leonardo DiCaprio plays the twins Philippe and Louis, and Gabriel Byrne plays D'Artagnan. Louis XIV is represented as a terrible ruler, while his brother Philippe is a much more likeable character. The Man in the Iron Mask is introduced as prisoner 64389000, the number of the mystery skeleton in the iron corset that Mirabeau had placed in the Bastille prison (see page 44).

Richard Chamberlain wears the mask in a 1977 British production.

FURTHER INFORMATION

IF YOU LIKED THIS BOOK, YOU MIGHT LIKE TO TRY
THESE OTHER GRAFFEX TITLES:

Treasure Island by Robert Louis Stevenson, Book House 2006
Oliver Twist by Charles Dickens, Book House 2006
Moby-Dick by Herman Melville, Book House 2007
The Hunchback of Notre Dame by Victor Hugo, Book House 2007
Kidnapped by Robert Louis Stevenson, Book House 2007
Journey to the Centre of the Earth by Jules Verne, Book House 2007
Dracula by Bram Stoker, Book House 2007

FOR MORE INFORMATION ON ALEXANDRE DUMAS:

en.wikipedia.org/wiki/Alexandre_Dumas
www.kirjasto.sci.fi/adumas1.htm
www.cadytech.com/dumas